African American
HOLIDAYS

James C. Anyike

A Historical
Research and Resource Guide
to Cultural Celebrations

Popular Truth, Inc.

Chicago, Illinois

Popular Truth, Inc.
334 East 37th Street
Chicago, IL 60653-1346

Library of Congress Catalog Card Number: 91-067532

ISBN: 0-9631547-0-2

Cover Design: Troy Brown Design, Chicago

Editing Assistance by Stephanie Gadlin

Manufactured in the United States of America

DEDICATION

To Dr. Carter G. Woodson for his life of commitment to popularizing the truth about the contributions and achievements of people of African descent.

TABLE OF CONTENTS

ACKNOWLEDGMENTS

Special Praise to the Most Gracious and Merciful Creator of the worlds and to His Word that allows me the privilege of a daily personal relationship with the Creator.

Special thanks to Bettie and Major Brame, my mother and father, for giving me manners, morals, values, culture and intellect, and to Lisa, my wife and queen, for extraordinary support and insight.

I warmly thank Rev. Walter McCray and Adrian Payton-Williams, for guiding my path in publishing this book, and Jawanza Kunjufu, Stephanie Gadlin, Rev. Melvin Jones, Dr. Anderson Thompson, Dr. Conrad Worrill, Rev. Willie B. Jemison, the staff of the Chicago Woodson Regional Library Vivian G. Harsh Research Collection, the King National Holiday Commission, the All-African People's Revolutionary Party, and the Association for the Study of Afro-American Life and History for valuable advice and information.

FOREWORD

As we approach the 21st century, it has become obvious that dangerous social trends, lack of good values, miseducation and moral degeneration threaten our hope for a bright future for generations of African Americans to come.

This book was written for individuals and institutions who are working to make a positive impact on the cultural, economic, political, educational, social and spiritual progress of present and future generations. Making progress is important to people of African descent in America. To improve life for future generations ought be the responsibility of every church, school, business, political caucus, and, especially, every family in the African American community.

The necessity of ethno-cultural celebrations to the progress of African Americans is evident. It is through our practice of celebrating African American holidays that we will instill in our people their culture, values, and morals, while simultaneously we popularize our history. The popularizing of *Dr. King's birthday, Black History Month*, and *Kwanzaa* have already begun the process of improving the self-esteem of our children, while dispelling historical misinformation so prevalent in our community.

Where there is no holiday there is no consecrated respect for the communal existence and values of a people. This book is written for all persons who seek to strengthen the culture, morals, values, and hopes of all African American people.

James C. Anyike
Chicago, IL

African American

HOLIDAYS

INTRODUCTION

When captives were taken from Africa to America, they were distinctly African. Almost four hundred years later, we are distinctly African American. We have gone from being called "African," to "Colored," to "Negroes," to "Black," to "Afro-Americans," to now being "African Americans." The designation "African American" indicates a great deal about our social development. It says that we are a people of African descent living in America as a distinct cultural body. This cultural body is made up of the collective experiences of all black people who have lived in America in the past and those who presently do. This culture is identified by jazz, blues, gospel and soul music; by modern dance and tap dancing; by hip talkin', pimp walkin', and high five passin'; by chicken fryin', chittlin' boilin', greens and cornbread makin', and pie bakin'; by sports playing, political campaigning, and nonviolent protesting; and rioting, oppression, lynching, and Black Power.

The word "holiday" historically means holy day, referring to a religious festival. The meaning now

1

includes secular celebrations also. Through the span of history people have always been grouped together based on tribal, regional, national, social and religious values. These values eventually lead to cultural distinctions that are often identified through special practices, beliefs and observances relevant to that group. Today's celebrations of certain holidays serve as opportunities to commemorate certain values and events, and to honor heroes and heroines of a specific group. Since African Americans are still evolving as a distinct group, we've only recently reached the point where African American holidays have gained popular support.

The African American holidays discussed are not holidays in the true sense of the word. Such is the case with Black History Month and Kwanzaa which are better defined as celebrations or special observances. This book was not meant to be a history book, though it has become historical in nature. This was unavoidable because the holidays discussed are a reflection of the evolution of African American people as a distinct body. Historical information has been presented to provide the reader with sufficient information on the historical context of these holidays. Also provided are perspectives on these holidays to better explain the relevance of these observances.

Chapter one is unlike the other chapters because it covers several holidays observed by slaves from the seventeenth century to the nineteenth century. It is interesting to note how important holidays were to the African in slavery, and to the slave owner as a tool to control the slave. Observances discussed in the chapter

2

are introduced to provide a foundation for the holidays discussed in the following chapters.

Chapter two discusses the National Observance of the birth of Dr. Martin Luther King, Jr., which is the only national holiday to honor an African American and the only one honoring an American other than George Washington. The enactment of this holiday into law is no small achievement.

Chapter three discusses Black History Month. The purpose of this month long observance is to bring attention to the many contributions and great achievements of black people throughout history.

Chapter four introduces the most recent effort in starting a new African American holiday, the National Malcolm X Day. Through this chapter the present value of Malcolm X to today's struggle for freedom is better understood.

Chapter five discusses the international observing of African Liberation Day. A description of the struggle for African people on the continent of Africa is provided. The reader will gain a better understanding of how the fight against colonialism in Africa is the same fight against white supremacy around the world.

Chapter six helps to dispel the popular misconception that the slaves preferred slavery and were heartbroken about leaving "the master" and his family. On the contrary, freed Africans responded to their legal emancipation with great excitement and celebration. This celebrating continues today and is popularly known as Juneteenth.

Chapter seven introduces Umoja Karamu, Kiswahili for "unity feast." The reader will learn the strength of unity and how it is to be celebrated each year.

Chapter eight describes the most important celebration of the African American holidays, Kwanzaa. This seven day observance focuses attention on seven important principles called the Nguzo Saba. The seven principles are Unity, Self-Determination, Collective Work and Responsibility, Cooperative Economics, Purpose, Creativity and Faith.

At the end of each chapter, except chapter one, information is provided on how to observe each holiday. This is important for those that wish to make these holidays a part of their annual calendar of events. These suggestions will establish a foundation for strong values, morals and culture for the home, school, church, business or civic organization.

The reader will find the treatment of this subject very informative, rich with cultural expression, and necessary for the uplifting of African people the world over. This can be the resulting impact when African American humanity is elevated and their culture is made popular.

Chapter 1

Slave Holidays

To better understand the holidays presently observed by African Americans, it is important to know the total history of celebrations and holiday observances among blacks since being brought to America in the 1600s. Holiday practices among slaves from the seventeenth to the nineteenth centuries provided the foundation for present day holiday practices by African Americans.

The history of holiday celebrations for blacks in America goes back as far as the formation of America as an independent power. On most plantations, blacks observed most of the holidays of the slave holder, such as Easter, the Fourth of July and Christmas. There were holidays specifically observed by blacks, with little or no participation from whites. Such holidays included the John Canoe Festival, the Pinkster Festival, and the Election Day celebration.

Other special events, that provided a welcomed break for blacks from rigorous plantation life were Saturday night parties, master's birthday, laying-by-crop jubilee, and rain or bad weather days. Slave holders considered these events and celebrations as important control mechanisms. According to Frederick Douglass, "holidays were among the most effective means in the hand of the slave holders of keeping down the spirit of insurrection among the slaves." However, he further concluded that if it were not for these holidays "the rigors of bondage would have become too severe for endurance, and the slave would have been forced to a dangerous desperation."[1] In spite of the motives of the slave holders, these celebrations provided a valuable opportunity for slaves to share their African culture in ways not so obvious to whites. Holidays and other special events allowed time for fellowship among the slaves. This time was used to sing songs, tell stories and hold dances in ways reminiscent of their African past. These celebrations facilitated the transmission of African culture from the old to the young.[2]

The excitement and enjoyment displayed by slaves at the Saturday night party, strongly contrasted the subdued attitude exhibited by them during the week. Many whites got the impression that their slaves were happy and content with their status as property of their master.[3] They did not understand that the slave was actually "laughing to keep from crying." Every Saturday night these parties were allowed on most plantations. The master usually provided the whiskey, and a chicken or pig for a barbecue. Some masters, and their families used these parties for their own amusement. Some liked to make the slaves drink until they were too drunk to stand. Others would make them fight like gladiators. Most masters left them alone to enjoy themselves. The occasional presence of whites was often considered an irritation, and was resented as an intrusion on what little time they had to enjoy themselves.[4]

Music for these parties was sometimes played on stringed instruments made from animal skins, horsehairs and animal bladders. In tune with the rhythm produced by percussion instruments made from tree logs and tin pans, they did a dance called the "Buzzard Lope." Other dances popular to them were "Cuttin'" the Pigeon's Wings," "Going to the East and Going to the West," and "Settin' de Flo."[5] Early curfews often ended these parties at nine o'clock, but, the slaves would re-start them after the overseer left. Unauthorized parties were sometimes held all night, deep in the forest away from the "big house." They would sometimes dance until dawn and still work a full day in the field.

Of the holidays observed by the slave holder, Christmas was the most important among slaves. It was not considered important for its religious content, but, because most slaves got four to six days off from their labor. Many of them used this as an opportunity to visit family members on other plantations, from which they had been separated. It was a time of gift giving, especially for the children. Some masters dispensed gift to the children dressed as Santa Clause.[6] Most slave masters gave small gifts to all of their slaves. The high point of Christmas for them was the partying that took place for several days, which included much eating, drinking, dancing, singing, courting and game playing. Many slaves celebrated their New Year's Day on December 28th, and on January 1st they began once again a new year in bondage. They dreaded the end of their Christmas celebration so much that they called New Year's Day "heart break day."

On most holidays observed by the slaveholders in the south, the slaves would usually celebrate by holding their own barbecues and parties near their quarters. In North Carolina these holidays provided an excellent opportunity for the appearance of John Canoe. On the streets of Wilmington, and several other North Carolina cities, John Canoe was a familiar sight on major holidays during the nineteenth century. He would always appear dressed in the most colorful costume, decorated with bits and pieces of material from a wide range of sources. Grass, colorful pieces of cloth, and animal skin are just a few of such sources. The white mask that he wore was usually described as "grotesque," often frightening to children and many adults. He sometimes wore a head piece shaped like a house or boat. He would dance down the street with a jerking, gyrating motion and would sing songs that told stories and tales. He also would accept contributions from people after his performance. He was sometimes accompanied by an assistant who would collect contributions, and would often be followed by a contingent of musicians and joyful followers as he led them in a Mardi Gras manner. This procession of merriment would last throughout the holiday and lead to a night of partying. It should be clearly understood that "John Canoe" was not the name of an individual, but the name of the costumed king that led the procession of a John Canoe Festival. This festival was the way that some North Carolina blacks made their fun on holidays observed by whites.

John Canoe, or Kunering, was known to have been performed in the eastern region of North Carolina (specifically, the towns of Edenton, New Bern,

8

Hillsboro, Wilmington, Hilton, Fayetteville and Southport). Kunering is still performed today in the West Indies, particularly in Jamaica and in Nassau.[7] There is little dispute that Kunering has its roots in Africa. Some believe John Canoe to be symbolic of "John Conny" the King of Axim on the Gold Coast of Africa. He outwitted Dutch merchantmen and maintained control of Fort Brandenburg, later rechristened "Conny's Castle."[8] According to the *Historical Dictionary of Ghana*, John Conny lived from 1660 to 1732 and was one of the great merchants on the Gold Coast in the early eighteenth century. From 1711 to 1724 he was commander of the Prussian fort of Gross Friedrichsburg (also called Fort Brandenburg) at Pokoso or Prince's Town, located 27 miles southwest of Takoradi.

For more than a decade John Conny facilitated trade between the Ashanti and Germans. He is most remembered and respected for holding off the Dutch from taking Fort Brandenburg for six years. He is sometimes called the "Last Prussian Negro Prince," and also the "Brandenburg Caboceer." The known variations in spelling the name given to this practice include "John Kooner," "Kunering," "John Kuner," "Who-Who's," "joncooner," "Jonkanoo," "John Connu," "John Conny," "John Crow," "Koo-Koo," "John Crayfish" "Jonkonnu, "Jonkeroo," and "John Canoe." Around 1900, Kunering was stopped by North Carolina police. It had also become unacceptable among some educated blacks that regarded it as degrading to the race.

The presence of king figures, like John Canoe, were a part of many festivals observed by African slaves.

Kunering is loosely associated with the Parade of Kings observed in Cuba and Election Day or Parade of Governors observed throughout New England.[9] New England slaves gathered in large numbers on holidays for public recreation and amusement. On one of these holidays they would hold an election to choose a governor that would serve as a respected authority figure over New England blacks. The election would then be followed by a major parade featuring their new governor. This practice began around 1750 and lasted about one hundred years. Thousands of slaves participated in parades held in Massachusetts, Rhode Island and Connecticut. After each parade, dinner and dancing would take place in a rented hall. The parade and dance were based on African culture, and the election format was based on the structure used by whites to elect their politicians. According to author Sterling Stuckey, "Blacks selected their best and ablest men as governors. Though the Negro governor had no legal power, he exercised, together with the lieutenant governor, justices of the peace, and sheriffs he sometimes appointed, considerable control over the Negroes throughout the state of Connecticut."[10]

Because many of those participating in the election were first generation Africans in America, the ethnicity (specific African heritage) of the candidate was an issue to the voters. At the end of the election any ill feelings that may have developed would be forgotten and the losing candidate would share the head table sitting at the right hand of the victor.

It is interesting to note that the appearance of king figures among slaves took place in states along the northeastern coastline of America. One reason could be that many of the Africans in these states are from the same region of Africa, and share similar customs. Another factor could be the cooperation of slave holders in allowing slaves to participate in these practices, allowing more flexibility for Africans to fraternize than southern plantation owners did.

In addition to North Carolina and New England, New York also had its king figure for blacks. He was known as the "Pinkster King." A celebration was conducted as a large festival on Pinkster Hill in Albany, New York. It was also known as "the Carnival of the African Race." The Pinkster festival lasted for seven days. This festival also included festive parades and all night dances. The Pinkster king was a respected man that may have been African royalty before being taken from Africa. His name was Charles and he was referred to as "King Charley." Charles was originally taken from Angola and was described as "tall, thin and athletic."[11] He was highly respected as the King of New York blacks until the last Pinkster Festival in 1811.

It also should be mentioned that in 1858 blacks in Boston began to observe March 5th as Crispus Attucks Day. It was on March 5, 1770 that Attucks and four others were shot by British soldiers. This commemoration was started as a protest against the Dred Scott Decision.[12] The observance was held at Faneuil Hall, where Attuck's remains lay.

On August 1, 1834, slavery was abolished by the British Parliament in their island colonies. This instilled a sense of hope among some blacks in America and they chose to observe August 1st as an independence celebration.   It also served as an alternative to the Fourth of July. The August lst celebration lasted until it was replaced with April 16th, the day that slavery was abolished in Washington D.C. in 1862. This observance was the closest forerunner to the emancipation celebrations, which are discussed in Chapter Six of this book.

The following chapters will deal specifically with African American holidays and celebrations which began after the abolishment of slavery and are currently being observed. These chapters are arranged according to their order on the calendar rather than chronologically.   This was done as a matter of convenience to those that will follow each event throughout the year. Close attention should be given to the instructions provided at the end of each of these chapters.   The instructions provided will give specific guidelines for observing each holiday.

Notes

----

1. Eugene D. Genovese, *Roll, Jordan, Roll,* (Random Houses Inc., New York, 1976) p. 577

2. Sterling Stuckey, *Slave Culture*, (Oxford University Press) p. 73

3. Genovese, *Roll, Jordan Roll*, p. 579

4. Ibid., p. 569

5. Ibid., p. 572

6. Ibid., p. 575

7. "The John Canoe Festival" *Phylon, The Atlanta University Review of Race and Culture*, Fourth Quarter 1942, p. 354

8. Ibid., p. 357

9. New England was a British colony and became the states of Rhode Island, Connecticuts New Hampshire, and Massachusetts.

10. Stuckey, *Slave Culture*, p. 77

11. Ibid., p. 81

12. "Historic Afro-American Holidays" by Benjamin Quarles, *Negro Digest*, February 1967, p. 15

Chapter 2

Martin Luther King's Birthday

(Third Monday of January)

I was five years old when Rev. Martin Luther King, Jr. was assassinated in 1968. Yet, I vividly remember watching the fires burning from our 9th floor apartment in Cabrini Green, a community of Chicago housing developments. I clearly remember seeing several groups of people marching through the community to show their pain and outrage that someone had so violently killed such a peaceful man. Riots had broken out in 120 cities in America. Many believed that the long awaited "Black Revolution" had come causing many African Americans to use whatever means necessary to strike out against "whitey" for killing Dr. King. Undoubtedly, Martin Luther King, Jr. stands out as a giant in the annals of African American history.

According to information gathered from the King Federal Holiday Commission, eight days after the assasination in Memphis, legislation was introduced by U.S. Representative John Conyers (D-MI) calling for a federal holiday honoring Dr. King. The bill failed to reach the House floor, but was reintroduced almost every session of Congress until it passed 15 years later. In 1971 Atlanta, Georgia, became the first city to designate Dr. King's Birthday as a paid holiday for city employees. In 1973 Illinois became the first state to declare January 15th a statewide holiday. Throughout the '70s and '80s, local government bodies across America honored Dr. King with proclamations, declarations of holidays, and by naming streets and schools in honor of him. The King Center For Nonviolent Social Change circulated petitions to gain broader support for a national holiday. More than six million people signed the petition. On January 15, 1981, which would have been Dr. King's 52nd birthday, more than 100,000 people met at the Washington Monument to rally for a national holiday led by Stevie Wonder and other national leaders.

On October 19, 1983, the U.S. Congress finally passed legislation making the third Monday of every January (beginning with 1986) the day America would honor Dr. King with a national holiday. In 1984 the Martin Luther King, Jr. Federal Holiday Commission was established by the government to help institute the holiday observance. The King Holiday is the tenth national holiday approved by Congress and the only one honoring an American other than George Washington. Attempts were made by Senator Jesse Helms (R-N.C.) to conduct a one-man filibuster and to use past charges of communist affiliations against Dr. King to tarnish his reputation. He then sued in federal court to have FBI files on Dr. King unsealed to determine whether the information in the files would prove Dr. King unworthy of a national holiday. The courts denied his motion, maintaining the fifty year seal placed on the files.[1]

According to author Taylor Branch, "The holiday owes something to a negative trend in contemporary race relations."[2] This "negative trend" included proposed tax exemptions for segregated schools, delaying an extension of the Voting Rights Act, and attacks on enforcement of affirmative action programs. Throughout the 1980s the Reagan and Bush administrations dismantled many of the civil rights and affirmative action gains of the 1960s and '70s. The nation watched as the definition of "minority" was expanded to include white women, the disabled and other ethnic groups. We also watched as the government cut back on the availability of grant and scholarship funding of educational programs for blacks. Branch contends that the conservative atmosphere of the early '80s required that the King holiday be yielded "as a political gesture, a throwaway holiday for Blacks." Despite the various political motives, the King holiday must be seen as an opportunity to strengthen the struggle for freedom, justice and self determination.

Examination of the life-history of Dr. King deserves a more in-depth analysis than provided here. This brief historical sketch provides enough information for us to appreciate Dr. King as a special person.

Dr. King's personal history is a great example of achievement. He entered Morehouse College at age 15, having skipped the 9th and 12th grades. He climbed the academic ladder and used education as an opportunity to develop his philosophies for social change, rather than only using it as a way to get a "good job" or make money. He was ordained into the ministry at 18 and received his Ph.D. from Boston University at the age of 26 in 1955. In December of that same year Rosa Parks refusal to give her bus seat to a white man in Montgomery, Alabama created an uproar. Consequently, a community meeting was held at the Dexter Avenue Baptist Church (where Dr. King had become Pastor in 1954) to discuss her arrest and plan the Montgomery Bus Boycott.

The many protests, sit-ins, boycotts, voter registration campaigns, marches and lobby campaigns led and inspired by Dr. King have proven the power of civil disobedience. However, the struggle to maintain the gains reached throughout the Civil Rights Movement has become a major issue that cannot be neglected. The failure to maintenance past gains and to use them as building blocks for further development has resulted in a collapse of the infrastructure of the movement. According to Rev. Jesse L. Jackson, Sr. "If Dr. King were alive and here today, he would be surprised that some of those who marched with him in life would be marching against him today."[3] The fact is, there are some civil rights leaders who have failed the movement. There are others who fear losing their community and political stature, so they will keep the movement in animated suspension. This type of leader has developed such a close relationship with those who they once had to boycott against, that they now have a vested interest in keeping those that are in power in the dominant position. Because we have failed to further develop collectively the African American communities economic resources, the economic strength gained by some parts of the African American community never circulate effectively to benefit the total community. The Southern Christian Leadership Conference (SCLC) began Operation Breadbasket to deal with this very issue.

During the latter years of his life, Dr. King's focus had become more national and international in scope. In March of 1967 he announced the need for the Civil Rights movement to develop a link with the Peace Movement in opposition to the Vietnam War and in November of that year, Dr. King announced plans for the SCLC Poor People's Campaign, hoping to bring attention to the plight of millions of American poor and disadvantaged. At the end of his life, Dr. King's nonviolence movement was losing its prominence to the Black Power Movement. Ironically, the murder of Dr. King released a wave of violent rioting, the very violence that he had worked for twelve years to prevent. The week of rioting that followed his murder was proof of the pain felt by African Americans in his passing.

Honoring Dr. King with a national holiday is proof of his significance to the American people. Dr. King's life and work extend beyond the perception of him as a man who "had a dream." He was a man that upset the comfort zone of American society. African Americans gained courage to sit at forbidden lunch counters, courage to drink from forbidden water fountains, and courage to vote in cities where one could be lynched for executing their legal rights. Many white Americans had

19

become so uncomfortable at seeing other whites killing and violently attacking blacks on their television and in newspapers throughout the country that their conscience would no longer allow them to maintain the many years of silence. He challenged all of America to work for change, and did not allow the repressive tactics of President Lyndon Johnson or J. Edgar Hoover to stop him. His message was to black people and white alike, cutting across lines of race.

Celebrating Dr. King's birthday must be done in respect of his sacrifice and should be observed according to his values. He spent his last birthday morning praying, eating breakfast, and talking with his family. At 10:00 a.m. he convened a group of his staff, advisors and supporters in the basement of the Ebenezer Baptist Church to plan for the Poor People's Campaign. This meeting included whites, Hispanics, African Americans, Native Americans, Asians, Jews, Protestants and Catholics. Rev. Jesse L. Jackson writes in *Straight From The Heart*, "Birthday celebrations must be appropriate to the person whose birthday it is.... Dr. King is a special kind of person who established how he wanted his birthday celebrated. You might recall that his request was basic: 'Just say I tried to help somebody'."[4]

In January of 1990 more than 500,000 people lined the streets of Atlanta to view the Martin Luther King, Jr. National Parade, sponsored by the King Federal Holiday Commission in cooperation with the Martin Luther King, Jr. Center for Nonviolent Social Change. In 1990 the holiday was officially observed by 44 American states, 4 U.S. territories and more than 100 nations around the world.

How to Celebrate
the King Holiday

Family Breakfast:

Symbolic of the breakfast that Dr. King shared with his family on January 15, 1968, families should conduct a special breakfast. This breakfast could involve the immediate family, other relatives, and special friends. The elder or someone designated by the elder of the family should bless the meal before it is served. Immediately following breakfast the family should convene a meeting to discuss the families health, economics and the future of the children.

Harambee:

Harambee is a Kiswahili word for pulling or coming together. It is symbolic of the meeting convened by Dr. King on his last birthday at the Ebenezer Baptist Church in Atlanta. Likewise harambee meetings should be held at churches, mosques and synagogues to discuss how the concerns of the poor and homeless will be addressed in the community or city that the religious institution hosting the harambee is located.

Community Action:

Some level of community action should be conducted on the 15th of January or on a day leading to the national observance. Such actions may include voter registration, protest at consulates or embassies of nations that have repressive policies, feeding of the homeless, boycotting companies that are unfair to workers or pollute the environment, letter writing campaigns to elected officials and student protest against institutional racism. These are just a few suggestions, the goal is to participate in some action rather than use this holiday merely as another day off from work.

Martin Luther King, Jr.
National Holiday Commission:

The National Holiday Commission, which is presently legislated to operate until 1994, has served as the leading force in shaping the observance of the King holiday. Through the leadership of Mrs. Coretta Scott King, who serves as its chairperson, a wide variety of activities are held and supported across the country in observance of the life of Dr. King.[5]

NOTES

----

1. "Behind the King Debate" *Newsweek Magazine*, October 31, 1983, p. 32

2. "Uneasy Holiday" by Taylor Branch, *The New Republic Magazine*, February 3, 1986, pp. 22-27

3. Rev. Jesse L Jackson, *Straight From The Heart* (Fortress Press, Philidelphia, 1987) p. 127

4. Ibid., p. 123

5. See Organization Listing on page 99.

Chapter 3

Black History Month

(Entire Month of February)

The words of Dr. Carter G. Woodson best describe the reasons for the inception of Negro History Week, which he started in 1926. In the October 1927 edition of the Journal of Negro History, Dr. Woodson stated the following:

> The celebration tends not to promote propaganda, but to counteract it by popularizing the truth. It is not interested so much in Negro History as it is in history influenced by the Negro; for what the world needs is not a history of selected races or nations but the history of the world void of national bias, race hate, and religious prejudice. There has been, therefore, no tendency to eulogize the Negro nor to abuse his enemies. The aim has been to emphasize important facts in the belief that facts properly set forth will speak for themselves.[1]

Dr. Woodson is the "Father of Black History." In 1915

he founded the Association for the Study of Negro Life and History (ASNLH) and the next year published the first edition of *The Journal of Negro History.*

The initiating of Negro History Week by Dr. Woodson is consistent with his commitment to institutionalizing the study and propagation of Black history. It was probably in November of 1925 that Dr. Woodson thought to begin this celebration. During this time, he communicated with other influential African Americans, all of which supported the idea. They then agreed on the second week of February for the observance of the achievements of the "Negro." This week was chosen because it is the week of the birthdays of Frederick Douglass and Abraham Lincoln, both highly respected at that time. Through the support of educators, ministers, and community leaders around the country, the first Negro History Week was a success. Each group and institution was left to its own initiative in working out a program particular to their local needs. This first observance included community speaker forums, discourses on Black history, and school plays portraying heroes in Black history. Special programs were also conducted by social welfare agencies, business organizations and recreational establishments. The celebration was generally observed by African Americans. However, there were integrated schools that participated.

During the 1960s the use of "Black" and "Afro-American" replaced the popular use of "Negro." At the 1972 Convention of the ASNLH, held in Cincinnati, Ohio, pressure from young delegates forced the organization to change its name to the Association for the Study of Afro-American Life and History (ASALH). Negro History Week was then changed to Black History Week. During America's Bicentennial celebration in 1976 the ASALH joined the nation in its focus on American history and decided to expand the observance of Black History Week to include the entire month of February. This was done to provide time for more activities focusing on the vast contributions of Blacks to the history of America. The observance was so successful that the Association decided to continue its monthly celebration.

The need for Black History Month has not diminished since the inception of Negro History Week in 1925. Dr. Woodson's rationale for the celebration remains relevant even into the 1990s. The contributions of African people continue to be misrepresented or not represented in history. Unfortunately, there are many white Americans who have greatly benefited from misinformation and lies about black people. The belief that the African was of an inferior race gave justification to chattel slavery. Through the use of slave labor, America was built largely by people who never reaped the benefits of even being recognized as citizens. Slavery created a tremendous disadvantage for black people mentally and economically. Yet, it created great benefits for whites and their descendants.[2] The debunking of religious, scientific, historical and philosophical misinformation about Blacks will continue into the 21st Century. The history of African Americans may one day become a recognized part of American heritage. Perhaps all American children will soon be taught about the great black athletes, scientists, inventors, artists, politicians, educators, entrepreneurs, explorers, ministers, and soldiers, just as black children are always taught of whites in these areas. A true and objective presentation of history eliminates the foundation of racism for some and increases the self-esteem of others. The observance of Black History Month must lead to the day when the history of the world will be void of national bias, race hate and religious prejudice.

How to Celebrate
Black History Month

African Heritage - 1st Week:

During the first week celebrations should focus on the contributions of Africans to world history. Attention must be given to the fact that all races came from African ancestors and that Kemet (Egypt) is the cradle of civilization. We must also remember how the wealth taken from Africa by colonial powers through exploitation of the people, minerals and land made the Western World powers quite rich. Our African heritage should be honored through our giving financial support to impoverished African nations and by supporting the anticolonial/anti-apartheid movements in Africa. By paying this tribute, we show our respect for our African heritage and our commitment to the future of the Mother Continent.

African Holocaust - 2nd Week:

During the second week memorial programs should be held to remember the tens of millions of Africans that died as a result of the slave trade. They died fighting against slavery in Africa, died in slave ships in the Middle Passage, died in chattel slavery, died revolting against slavery in America, died from lynching and they died in race riots that have taken place in hundreds of American cities. Families must honor the memory of their known and unknown ancestors that died in America. The children of the family must be told about their ancestors that have already passed on, especially those that died fighting for freedom.

Great Heroes and Heroines - 3rd Week:

During the third week we must pay tribute to the many men and women of distinction in Black history. We must remember the great abolitionists, inventors, scientists, entrepreneurs, athletes, artists, entertainers, ministers, soldiers, and others of our past. Children should portray their heroes and heroines by acting in plays and skits. Adults could have fun honoring theirs by holding costume parties and dressing in the likeness of their heroes and heroines.

Rites of Passage - 4th Week:

The last week should be used as an opportunity for the men and women of the community to conduct Rites of Passage Programs for the young men and women. This is a process of taking youth into adulthood by training them on their history, morals, values, sexuality and responsibilities to their family. This training may be designed to pass on family, religious, and cultural values. The training should be segregated by sex and the youth should be sixteen (or approaching sixteen within the year). The passage may take several hours or even days. At the completion of the rites, these new adults should be given something of value to signify their passing into adulthood.[3]

NOTES

----

1. "Annual Report of The Director" *Journal of Negro History*, October 1927, p. 573

2. Eric Williams, *Capitalism and Slavery*, (University of North Carolina Press, 1944) p. 6

3. Refer to the *African American Holiday Supply Kit* information for rites of passage guidelines on page 101.

Chapter 4

National Malcolm X Day

(May 19)

In 1990 the effort to organize the National
Malcolm X Day observance became a major thrust of
the African American Progressive Action Network
(AAPAN). Local observances have been maintained in
Philadelphia for 9 years by Sisters Remember Malcolm
and in Washington D.C. Malcolm X Celebrations have
been held for more than 20 years. The AAPAN formed
the National Malcolm X Commemoration Commission
Steering Committee (NMXCC) to organize an effort to
rally support for the national observance. The
Malcolm X Commemoration is the most recent
organized event of the African American holidays
described in this book. The life and example of
Malcolm X deserve our respect and appreciation. His
life history is a comprehensive picture depicting the
experiences of different segments of the African
American society. The changes that he had experienced
took him from the lowest of the black social strata to the
highest. Therefore, the relevance of the Malcolm X

Commemoration lies within understanding the history of Malcolm X.

During his lifetime, Malcolm X had been referred to by different names at different points in his life. He was born Malcolm Little on May 19, 1925 in Omaha, Nebraska. His father was a Baptist preacher and organizer for the Universal Negro Improvement Association which was founded by Marcus Garvey in 1911. Malcolm Little had a very troubled childhood. His father was killed for trying to organize blacks in Michigan and his mother became mentally ill due to the strain of raising a family during the Great Depression. In the Autobiography of Malcolm X, Malcolm recalls a conversation that he had with his 8th grade English teacher. The teacher asked him if he had been thinking about a career? Malcolm replied "Well, yes sir, I've been thinking I'd like to be a lawyer." His teacher responded by saying "But you've got to be realistic about being a nigger. A Lawyer, that's no realistic goal for a nigger." He then encouraged Malcolm to plan on being a carpenter, because he was good with his hands. Malcolm recalls that the more he thought about it, the more "uneasy" it made him and that it was then that he began to "change inside"[1] After his mother was institutionalized, his family was split up among relatives and foster homes.

At age 16 Malcolm moved to New York City, where he became known as "Detroit Red." He found work shining shoes, working on a commuter train, and as a waiter. "Red" eventually became a full time hustler, after being fired by a restaurant for finding a prostitute for a customer. During this time in his life, he lived like many of today's African American youth. He was unskilled and a school drop out. He tried a few legal employment opportunities, but later, found it easier to take advantage of the many illegal employment opportunities. These same illegal opportunities continue to lure tens of thousands of our youth into a cycle of criminal activity. "Red" sold drugs, pimped and became a dope addict. He committed armed robbery and burglary to support his drug habit.[2]

In 1946 Malcolm was convicted of burglary and sentenced to a 10 year prison term. By this time Malcolm was a hard, bitter man. The other inmates considered him so mean that they nicknamed him "Satan." This was probably the lowest point in his life. However, it was within those prison walls that he began to rebuild his life. The Malcolm that entered Charlestown State Prison in 1946 would not be the same Malcolm to leave prison six years later. While in prison, he was introduced to the Islamic teachings of the Honorable Elijah Muhammad. Malcolm was attracted by Elijah's teaching that the white man was the "devil." He felt that this explained why he had such a hard, painful life.[3] This belief lifted the self-blame and low self-esteem from him and left the blame with the "white devil." In Malcolm's mind, his life of trouble began to make sense. This "devil "became the reason his father was killed, why his mother was ill, why he was uneducated, why crime was the most obvious option for him and why he was now in prison. He then pledged to Allah that he would "tell the black man the true teachings of Islam and the white man the truth about his crimes."

Malcolm began to improve his vocabulary by memorizing the words in a dictionary. He also took correspondence courses in English and Latin. Most importantly, he would regularly correspond with his teacher the Honorable Elijah Muhammad. He had become so strong in his faith that he led prison study groups on Islam. In 1952 Malcolm was paroled and lived with his brother Wilfred. During this time he worked for a furniture company, an automobile manufacturer and continued to study Islam in Detroit Temple No. 1, where he received his "X." In 1953 Malcolm was appointed Assistant Minister of Temple No. 1 and later as Elijah Muhammad's Prime Minister throughout the United States. Malcolm went on to organize Nation Of Islam (NOI) mosques in Boston, Philadelphia, New York, Atlanta, and Los Angeles.

In 1958 Malcolm married Sister Betty X and together they had six daughters. As a husband, he was devoted, loving, and affectionate to his wife. Despite his tarnished past, Malcolm X became the "Prince of the Black Revolution." His love for African people and the strength that he showed was an inspiration to thousands of people. In 1964, after he left the Nation Of Islam, there were many more threats on his life. In response to a reporters question regarding him being concerned about these threats, Malcolm said "I don't worry ... I believe that I'm a man that died 20 years ago (referring to his past addiction and crimes), and I live like a man who is dead already. I have no fear whatsoever, of anybody or anything."[4] It was this courage that inspired Black Militancy among youth of the 60s. The undying message of rights by "the ballot or the bullet" and freedom "by any means necessary" still inspire a new generation of youth. Malcolm's message instilled boldness in African people, giving us courage to confront racist violence with violent retaliation. It was this boldness that challenged the centuries of fear that African Americans held of white people.

Malcolm X was assassinated on February 21, 1965 by three black men while addressing an audience at the Audubon Ballroom in Harlem. He just begun a new chapter in his life as El Hajj Malik El Shabazz, founder of Muslim Mosque Inc. and the Organization of African-American Unity. In his last year, he began to spread the understanding that the oppression of African Americans was an issues of human rights, instead of civil rights. As an issue of human rights, Malcolm intended to appeal to the World Court on behalf of oppressed Blacks.

More than 25 years after Malcolm's assasination, his reputation as the Prince of the Black Revolution remains firm. In the late 1980s a new generation of youth began to become familiar with Malcolm's teachings through such rap music artist as Public Enemy. Today's black community can learn much from Malcolm's life. His life is a symbol of hope for every fatherless child, because he was fatherless; for every thug on our city streets, because he was a thug; and for every prisoner, because he was in prison. He is a symbol of manhood as a loving faithful husband and good father to his children. He was a great minister that, like Jesus, went to the low places of the society to take his people to a higher level. He was a great leader that did not compromise his values to satisfy the selfish motives of others that sought to take advantage of African people. He was a great servant because he gave his life for us.

In 1990 thousands of people signed petitions circulated by the NMXCC to state their support for the National Malcolm X Day, held every May 19th. Unlike the King holiday, this observance is for black people to honor a man that primarily concerned himself with black issues. The NMXCC does not seek to have the government approve this observance, they only seek the support of people of African descent.

How to Celebrate

National Malcolm X Day

The NMXCC recommends that an international conference be held to extend the Malcolm X initiative throughout the Pan African world. They further recommend that local commemoration commissions be established in cities across America. The following information may also provide direction on observing National Malcolm X Day.

National "We Remember Malcolm Day":

The NMXCC suggest that the date of Malcolm's assasination, February 21st, be observed to build up to the more important May 19th observance. The NMXCC plans to use this date to hold national symposiums, poster contests and rap contests. College Campuses are also encouraged to conduct these types of programs.

Displays and Portraits:

Homes, schools, businesses and other institutions should honor this day by setting up a display. This display can be a portrait, tribute, or banner acknowledging support for National Malcolm X Day.

Prison Outreach:

Due to the high number of blacks in American prisons and jails, most African Americans know at least one individual that is presently incarcerated. It was Malcolm's brother that introduced him to Islam, which changed his life. Malcolm proved that prison does not have to be the end of life. Therefore, we should not give up on our brothers and sisters that are in prison. We should observe this day by visiting those who we know are in prison or by sending a letter of encouragement.

Street Outreach:

Malcolm was successful in spreading Islam and increasing the membership of the Nation Of Islam because he walked the streets where the people needed him most. Malcolm's ministry was for the highly moral and reprobate alike. Likewise, ministers and leaders should observe this day by spreading their message to the most forsaken of our society in the innercities and southern hamlets of America.

Support Human Rights For Black People:

Malcolm did not have the opportunity to appear before the World Court regarding human rights for black people, as he planned. This important task can still be accomplished by sending letters and petitions to the World Court and United Nations. These communiques should address specific cases of exploitation, miseducation, murder, experimentation, false imprisonment, disenfranchisement, or any human rights violation against African people around the world.

NOTES

1.
Malcolm X and Alex Haley, *Autobiography of Malcolm X*, (Grove Press, New York, 1964) pp. 36-37

2. Ivan Van Sertima and Clifton E. Marsh, *Great Black Leaders: Ancient and Modern*, (Journal of African Civilization Ltd., Inc., 1988) pp. 77-78

3. "*Malcolm X,*" Documentary produced by Marvin Worth and Arnold Perl, distributed by Warner Bros.

4. Ibid.

Chapter 5

African Liberation Day

(May 25th)

African Liberation Day (ALD) is a celebration unlike most holidays . Rather than seeking to commemorate some great day of the past when "African liberation" was won, this is an observance which focuses attention on a future goal of African liberation. Most holidays are set to acknowledge great individuals of the past or to commemorate great past events. We cannot yet celebrate African liberation, because all African people are not yet free. We celebrate ALD as a day to emphasize our oneness in the struggle to end European domination and white supremacy.

The ALD observance began at the Conference of Independent African States in Accra, Ghana April 15, 1958, hosted by Prime Minister Osageyfo Kwame Nkrumah of Ghana. Those attending the conference represented the governments of the first African nations to gain independence in Africa. The conference delegates passed a resolution declaring April 15th African Freedom Day (AFD). This observance would mark the progress of the liberation movement each year and serve as a symbol of the African's determination to free themselves from colonialism and foreign exploitation. Between 1958 and 1963 AFD was supported around the world by a wide range of leaders. Among the African leaders to support this observance were Emperor Haile Selassie of Ethiopia, Julius Nyerere of Tanzania, President Seku Ture of Guinea, Kenneth Kaunda of Zambia, Patrice Lumumba of the Congo and many others. American support included Malcolm X, President John F. Kennedy, Senator Hubert Humphrey and the Chicago based Afro-American Heritage Association.[1]

The end of World War II marks an important period in the thrust for African liberation. Following the war the British Empire was weak economically and could not maintain control of their vast empire. The challenge to British colonialism in India, led by Mahatma Gandhi, provided an example for African nationalist movements.[2] Through uprisings and negotiated settlements, British colonies in Africa gained their independence. Uprisings in the Belgian Congo (now Zaire) in 1959 forced Belgium to grant independence in 1960. Fighting in the French colony of Algeria lasted from 1954 to 1962 when Algeria gained its independence. The year 1960 was declared the "Year of Africa" because 17 African countries gained their independence during this time. Some of the great African leaders who led the African nationalist movement include Kwame Nkrumah in Ghana, Patrice Lumumba in the Congo, and Sekou Toure in Guinea. It was also during this time that the Civil Rights Movement in America was experiencing some of it's greatest successes.

On May 25, 1963 thirty-one independent African countries met to form the Organization of African Unity (OAU). At this historic meeting the delegates changed African Freedom Day into African Liberation Day and chose May 25th as the new date for the observance. Each year's observance of ALD brought reports of victories and defeats against colonialism. Throughout the 60s ALD was observed widely in Africa. Observances were also held in the USSR, Brazil, Canada, and the United States. In 1972, more than 40,000 people participated in ALD in Washington D.C., and 10,000 participated in San Francisco.

The concept of "African liberation" poses some problems that must be addressed in order to better understand the relevance of ALD. In spite of the fact that most African nations gained independence after World War II, they did not gain liberation from the economic, educational, religious and ideological systems that have kept them dependent on imperialist powers. European nations, in many cases, granted independence in return for mineral rights, control of land, parliamentary positions and freedom to operate businesses tax free.[3] African leaders held the seats of government, but, the Europeans maintained much control and influence. Over four centuries of colonialism left Africans with European forms of language, education, religion and government.

African Americans experienced the same fate after slavery was abolished by the Congress of the United States in 1865, many blacks remained economically,

45

religiously, and ideologically connected to their former masters. Years of slavery resulted in a great dependency on a racist American society, by oppressed blacks. Though many African nations gained independence, years of colonialism led to dependency on the Western World economic system, in which African nations are taken advantage of.

The economic concern is not the only problem posed to African liberation, history also poses problems. Historically, African people did not view themselves from a continental point of view. They defined themselves according to regional, cultural and tribal differences within the continent of Africa. The grouping of all black Africans, was done from the European perspective. In 1884 the Berlin Conference was held by European colonial powers to decide how Africa would be split up between the nations (Britain, France, Germany, Portugal, Belgian, Spain and Italy). A rush for gold and other precious minerals heated up as the slave trade cooled down. Most of the boundaries drawn during this period of colonialism still exist as the boundaries for present African nations. Therefore, the forming of many African countries originated from colonialism, which had no respect for regional, tribal or cultural boundaries already maintained by precolonial African people. These tribal differences did not disappear after colonization began and they continue to cause tribal conflicts that impede African unity. The whole of the African continent has been defined from a European point of view by cartographers, drawing Africa disproportionately smaller and putting Europe above the African continent. Many African nations have changed their names as a key step towards anticolonialism and self-determination.

The last major bastion of European domination in Africa is the South African government. World attention has been given to the racist apartheid system and the violence used by the South African government against black South Africans. The country is structured to provide a paradise for it's 5 million white citizens, while the 23 million blacks suffer. In 1990 the South African government abolished passbook laws, freed African National Congress (ANC) leader Nelson Mandela and in 1991 introduced legislation to end separate public accommodations. These and other changes have been viewed as "too much" by many white South Africans, while considered "not enough" by most black South Africans. Major change in the country may not come until all citizens have equal voting rights. This may then be followed by a fair distribution of the land, of which whites presently control 87 percent and blacks are left with 13 percent of the countries less desirable land. A new South African government will find it necessary to implement an active plan to develop better political, educational and economical opportunities for it's black citizens. Liberation in South Africa may someday mean Africans gaining control of the mineral wealth that has made the country one of the riches in the world. The African continent has the potential to yield enough food and mineral wealth to eliminate hunger and poverty among poor African countries.

African Liberation Day is important as an African American holiday. Because, the source of African colonialism and African American oppression are the same source, Western World economic interest. The economic interest of European nations produced racism, slavery, colonialism and exploitation of African people and raw materials. It is the monetary system of this economic interest that Black people are subject to all over the world. Therefore, blacks are subject to the same racism, oppression and exploitation around the world. The question of African liberation is a Pan-African one. As blacks in one part of the world gain greater liberation, others around the world feel the impact. Likewise, the Civil Rights Movement of the 1960s greatly inspired the liberation movement in South Africa. Also, the economic growth of African nations has increased international trade between African and African American businesses in the 80s.

The All African People's Revolutionary Party (AAPRP),[4] most notably represented by one of its key organizers, Kwame Ture (formerly Stokely Carmichael), has served as a major force in observing ALD around the world. The AAPRP has conducted symposiums, conferences and marches each year, attracting thousands of participants. According to Dr. Conrad Worrill, President of the National Black United Front, ALD events are also sponsored by NBUF chapters in Houston, Detroit, San Francisco, Chicago and many other American cities.

How to Celebrate
African Liberation Day

Most ALD observances around the world involve public marches, parades, and rallies. These events are usually held to celebrate victories won against colonialism, to inform the masses of black people about the status of the liberation movement, and to inspire greater determination in fighting against oppression. The following suggestions may also enhance the ALD observance:

African Support Funds:

Financially supporting poor African countries and various liberation movements is an excellent way to observe ALD. African freedom will not come without substantial financial support. Such support would go to organizations working for black empowerment in Africa, America, or anywhere in the world where we are oppressed. Prior to extending support to any person or organization, you should verify their validity to assure proper use of your support.

Red, Black, and Green:

Marcus Garvey, founder of the Universal Negro Improvement Association, chose the colors red, black, and green to symbolize the Black Nationalist Movement and flag. Red is a symbol of the blood shed by millions of Africans, black is symbolic of our race, and green symbolizes our motherland, Africa. We could display these colors on ALD together by wearing clothing of this color scheme, displaying the red, black and green flag, or by displaying red, black and green ribbons on our cars or clothing.

The AAPRP uses a different color symbol. On African Liberation Day it asks its participants to wear all white to symbolize monolithic unity, and to send a message of solidarity among all African people.

Parades, Marches, Rallies, and Conferences:

You may also contact local organizations for information on ALD events in your area. Black owned bookstores often are informed about activities. You may contact the All-African People's Revolutionary Party and the National Black United Front for information on parades, rallies, marches, and conferences being held for ALD.[5]

NOTES

----

1. "Thirty Years of African Liberation Day" Pamphlet, Prepared By the All-African People's Revolutionary Party, 1988, pp. 4-6

2. Ali A. Mazrui, *The Africans*, (Little, Brown and Company, Boston and Toronto, 1986) pp. 178-180

3. Kwame Nkrumah, *Africa Must Unite*, (International Publishers, New York, 1970) pp. 174-175

4. In contrast to the terms "Black" or "African American," the AAPRP exclusively uses the term "African" to indicate the identity of people of African ancestry all over the world.

5. See Organization Listing on page 99.

Chapter 6

Juneteenth
National Freedom Day

(June 19th)

This celebration of freedom from slavery is the oldest African American holiday observance. Unlike the other holidays, Juneteenth observances began spontaneously throughout the country. The other holidays were started by specific individuals and organizations at a specific time and place. This celebration is known by many names, such as "Emancipation Day," "Emancipation Celebration," "Freedom Day," "Jun-Jun," and "Juneteenth." For reasons that will be explained in this chapter, I prefer to call this observance Juneteenth National Freedom Day (hereafter referred to simply as Juneteenth). Words cannot adequately express the great joy that erupted among blacks when they learned of their freedom. It was a great feeling of rapture and it resulted in great celebrations all across America. The reporting of these celebrations have been ignored in mainstream history. The only book on this subject that I know is *O Freedom! Afro-American Emancipation Celebrations* by William H. Wiggins, Jr., which provides an excellent body of knowledge on Juneteenth. We are often given the impression that the slave loved his master so much that it broke his heart that he was set free. However, Juneteenth stands as positive proof that the slave hated slavery and celebrated its abolishment with excitement.

Chattel slavery in America was the most cruel and inhumane form of slavery in history. It began in 1441 when Portuguese men, under the command of Antam Goncalvez, captured slaves south of the Sahara to present to their prince.[1] As the slave trade developed, Europeans developed a preference of capturing slaves from West African societies that were accustomed to agricultural labor and sedentary habits. Therefore, most of those brought to North America were from the Igbo, Ewe, Biafada, Bakongo, Wolof, Bambara, Ibibio, Serer, and Arada tribes.[2] Slaves were stacked in the bottoms of slave ships for a month long journey across the Atlantic Ocean called the "Middle Passage." It is estimated that eleven to twelve million Africans survived this voyage to the "New World."[3] The number of those that died fighting against the slave trade in Africa and those that died in the Middle Passage is unknown, but, is likely more than those that survived the ocean voyage.

The Middle Passage was a painful journey. In the bottom of these ships, the slaves would be packed together among human waste, rats, and the smell of death from decomposing flesh. They were subjected to whippings, castration, branding and rape as slaves in

America. For more than 200 years, they were forced to submit to slavery and they prayed, cried, fought and died for the day that they would be free.

The New Teachers' and Pupils' Cyclopedia says the following about the rift between the North and South which led to the Civil War in 1861: "Sectional differences had existed from the beginning of the Union, but after the time of the Missouri Compromise of 1820 the differences were based largely upon the economic and social divergence between the North and the South caused by the existence of slavery. Frequent tendencies to disrupt the government prevailed from time to time, but they increased materially after 1850, chiefly on account of the passage of the Fugitive Slave Law and incidents connected with its enforcement. Other causes of dissatisfaction were the repeal of the Missouri Compromise in 1854, the Dred Scott Decision of the United States Supreme Court in 1858, the Lecompton Constitution for Kansas in 1858, and the John Brown raid at Harper's Farry in 1859. However, the election of Lincoln in 1860 brought disunion to a head."[4]

Concerning the 1860 Presidential Election between Lincoln and Douglas, Booker T. Washington wrote, "every slave on our plantation felt and knew, though other issues were discussed, the primal one was that of slavery." Between December, 1860 and March, 1861 seven southern states seceded from the Union, they were Alabama, Florida, Georgia, Louisiana, Mississippi, South Carolina and Texas. On February 4, 1861 The Confederate States of America were formed. Later in 1861, North Carolina, Arkansas, Virginia and Tennessee joined the Confederacy.

The discussion of freedom among slaves was consistent throughout the history of slavery in America. The growing anticipation of their ultimate liberation continued to swell when the Civil War began in April, 1861 with the Confederate attack on Fort Sumter. In 1862, the first clear signs of the end of slavery were realized when laws were passed abolishing slavery in the territories (Oklahoma, Nabraska, Colorado and New Mexico) and in Washington, D.C. On August 22, 1862, President Lincoln stated, "My paramount object is to save the Union, and not either to save or destroy slavery. If I could save the Union without freeing one slave I would do it." On September 22, 1862, President Lincoln issued a proclamation notifying the rebellious states that if they did not return to the Union by January 1, 1863, he would declare their slaves "forever free." This led to the celebrated Emancipation Proclamation which declared slaves of the eleven rebel states free. Lerone Bennett, Jr. writes in *Before the Mayflower* about the great anticipation of the New Years Eve before the proclamation was delivered. According to Bennett, "that night, Negroes gathered in churches and prayed the Old Age out and the New Age in. There was no doubt about what Lincoln would do at the watch meeting." However, Bennett describes the doubt of many of those awaiting an official announcement at the Tremont Temple in Boston, where Frederick Douglass and many others waited throughout the day for this historic moment. When the announcement finally came across the telegraph wires "suddenly, everyone was on his feet shouting, laughing, and weeping." The next day, after much of the excitement had passed and Douglass and others more carefully examined the proclamation, Bennett states that they "were disappointed," because the document lacked the literary aesthetics of other statements and documents delivered by President Lincoln. They were also disappointed because it did not free all who were in slavery in America. Lincoln considered the declaration an act of "military necessity." The President's proclamation also urged the former slaves to restrain from violence against their former masters and extended an invitation for the newly freed men to join the Union military and Navy. Enforcement of the Emancipation Proclamation took place in rebel states where the Union Army gained control.

The newly freed Africans responded with great excitement when freedom reached their plantations. Throughout America, Juneteenth is observed on different dates because enforcement of their liberation would come only after the defeat of local Confederate forces. On January 31, 1865, Congress passed the Thirteenth Amendment abolishing slavery throughout all of the United States and areas subject to its jurisdiction. This amendment was necessary, because the Emancipation Proclamation did not outlaw slavery throughout the whole country, but, only in the eleven states that seceded from the Union. The war ended with the surrender of the Army of the Northern Virginia on April 9, 1865. For many years slaves were told that their freedom would come in the "next world," now most of them knew it would come within days in this world. Booker T. Washington writes in *Up From Slavery* that "word was sent to the slave quarters to the effect that something unusual was going to take place at the "big house" the next morning. There was little, if any, sleep that night. All was excitement and expectancy." Washington recalls that when they were informed of their freedom, the next morning, "there was great rejoicing, and thanksgiving, and wild scenes of ecstasy. But there was no feeling of bitterness."[5]

June 19, 1865 was the day that the message of freedom reached Texas blacks. This is where the popular name "Juneteenth" (for June 19th) comes from. The following dates indicate when Juneteenth was, or is, observed in certain states. Each specific date may be an indication when the message of freedom reached different parts of the country.[6]

January 1st - New York City*, Boston*, Alabama, Georgia, North Carolina, South Carolina, Virginia, Tennessee, Maryland

February 1st - Philadelphia

May 8th - Eastern Mississippi

May 20th - Florida

June 19th - East Texas, Oklahoma, Louisiana, Southwestern Arkansas, Southern Oklahoma, California*

August 1st - Ontario (Canada)*

August 4th - Northeastern Arkansas, Northcentral Tennessee, Central Oklahoma, Southeastern Missouri, Southwestern Illinois

August 8th - Southwestern Kentucky

September 22nd - Indiana, Illinois, Ohio

* - indicates that the Juneteenth observance was probably brought to the state by observers from another state.

The freedom message reached different parts of America on various dates between 1863 and 1865. Texas slaves were not informed about the Emancipation Proclamation that freed them in 1863, until after the Civil War ended in 1865. Celebrations in Canada, northern states and California were brought to these locations as southern blacks migrated to other parts of the country.

The National Freedom Day observances held in Philadelphia on February 1st originated through the efforts of Mr. R.R. Wright, Sr. It was on February 1st that Lincoln signed the Thirteenth Amendment. Wright succeeded in getting President Harry Truman to declare February 1st "National Freedom Day."[7] The celebration of freedom is more than 130 years old and will continue as long as its observance is passed on to new generations.

Calling this observance "Juneteenth National Freedom Day" is done to use the already familiar title "Juneteenth" as a reference and "freedom" is used to describe the motive for the celebration as it relates to when all Africans in America gained their legal freedom. Therefore, the word "freedom" has more relevance on a national scale than "emancipation." I recommend that June 19th be recognized as the date for JNFD for the sake of uniformity. Local observances should continue to be held on the dates common to that region. June 19th, nevertheless, can be a date of national importance to African Americans as we share in the celebration. The Chicago Black United Community (CBUC), founded by Lu Palmer, conducts its observances during June to take advantage of the good weather and to symbolize the time of year when summer "frees" us from the limitations of the cold of winter. Juneteenth celebrations often include picnics, parties, church services, talent contest, beauty pageants, sports events, breakfast meetings, luncheons, and dinners. There are many different ways to enjoy the day that brought joy to our ancestors.

How to Celebrate
Juneteenth National Freedom Day

Reading of Freedom Documents:

Many regions read the Emancipation Proclamation, the Thirteenth Amendment, or a local declaration honoring freedom from slavery. This is an appropriate way to begin JNFD, which is also symbolic of the day when our ancestors stood in front of the "big House" to be informed of their legal freedom.

Celebrate:

This should be a day of fun, food, family, music and dancing. We can observe this day with great joy, as our ancestors did. This is not done to ignore the many problems that we must still confront in order to have full freedom. It is done to express our joy for how far we've come. The key word for this day should be "fun." A family picnic, games, dancing and singing are all acceptable on this day.

NOTES

----

1. Basil Davidson, *The African Slave Trade*, (Atlantic Little, Brown and Company, Boston/Toronto, 1980) p. 53

2. John W. Blassingame, *The Slave Community*, (Oxford University Press, New York, 1975) p. 2

3. Davidson, *The African Slave Trade*, pp. 96-97

4. "Civil War In Americas," *The New Teachers' and Pupils' Cyclopedia*, Vol. II, (The Holst Publishing Company, 1919) p. 589

5. Booker T. Washington, *Up From Slavery*, (A Bantam Book/Published by arrangement with Doubleday & Company, Inc., 1977) pp. 13-14

6. William H. Wiggins, Jr., *O Freedom! Afro-American Emancipation Celebrations*, (University of Tennessee Press) pp. xviii-xix

7. Ibid., p. 20

Chapter 7

Umoja Karamu

(4th Sunday of November)

Though I have seven brothers and sisters, I didn't realize the full significance of family until I had my own. Being a responsible father to one son has given me tremendous respect for my parents raising eight children. As an adult, I can now appreciate the strength and unity of my family. Many African American families are failing in many ways. Some couples have chosen divorce, abandonment, violence, and adultery, rather than communication, forgiveness, perseverance, and unity. In today's society, a family member or friend may be more likely to kill you than a stranger is. The chance of me being shot by another African American man far outweigh the chances of a racist white man taking my life. We are losing our understanding of the value of family unity. In many of today's families, past disputes have resulted in years of bitter feelings. Family gatherings sometimes turn into shouting and shooting matches. I now completely understand how blessed I am to have a family that I love and like.

Minister Louis Farrakhan, of the Nation Of Islam, once said, "marriage begins the process of two people striving to become one." Marriage is often misunderstood to be the final step of a couple developing a relationship. However, it is the first real step for a couple. It is then that we vow to "love and honor," for "richer or poorer," through "sickness and health." This is a promise to struggle together as a lifetime commitment. This is what unity is all about. Unity is a commitment to strive together in harmony. The commitment of the African American family to strive together in harmony, an important dimension of unity, is an important part of our heritage and history. It is from this spirit that the Umoja Karamu is to be observed.

"Umoja" and "karamu" are kiswahili words, which together mean "unity feast." This celebration was founded by Bro. Edwards Simms, Jr. and introduced as a holiday for African Americans in 1971. That year, it was observed in Philadelphia and Washington D.C. It was the Temple of the Black Messiah in Washington D.C. that established the fourth Sunday of November as the date for the Umoja Karamu. According to Brother Simms, "the Umoja Karamu, a ritual for the Black Family, has been developed as an effort to inject new meaning and solidarity into the Black Family through ceremony and symbol."[1]

The ceremony of the Umoja Karamu is based on five periods of African American life. Each period is represented by a specific color to be used in the ceremony. The first period is the Black Family as it was before slavery in Africa and is portrayed by the color black. The second period is the Black Family in slavery and is portrayed by the color white. The third period is the emancipated Black Family, portrayed by the color red. The fourth period is the Black Family struggle for liberation, portrayed by the color green. The fifth, and final, period is the Black Family look to the future, represented by the color orange or gold. During the ceremony, narratives on each period will be read as music common to each era will be played. Five separate color foods also will be used to represent each period.

Today, the Umoja Karamu is celebrated in churches and homes in several states (i.e. Maryland, Pennsylvania, Illinois, and Washington D.C.). Though it has not yet reached the popularity of Kwanzaa, its relevance to today's Black Family is great.

How to Celebrate
The Umoja Karamu

The Umoja Karamu celebration described herein is based on the outline given by Rev. Ishakamusa Barashango.[2]

State of Mind:

The mindset of those participating in the Umoja Karamu ritual should be of faith, hope, and love for the Black Community. Therefore, anyone in conflict with another person in attendance should seek to reconcile their problem before participating. Also, those lacking faith in the future of the African American community should seek to restore their faith.

Home Observance:

A table should be set with five different colored foods representing the following five periods:

  1st Period - The Black Family in Africa before slavery, represented by food the color black (i.e., blackeye peas).
  2nd Period - The Black Family in slavery, represented by food that is white (i.e., rice).
  3rd Period - The Black Family after emancipation,

represented by the color red (i.e., tomatoes).

4th Period - The Black Family in struggle for liberation, represented by the color green (i.e., greens).

5th Period - The Black Family hoping for the future, represented by the color orange or gold (i.e., sweet potatoes or corn). These foods should be placed on a table and covered with a tablecloth overlaid with a red, black and green flag or African print material. It will remain covered until the unity ritual begins. A bowl of water and a clean towel must be placed on the table, so that between each serving of food the person conducting the ritual can wash his/her hands. The washing is done to express the sacredness of the ritual.

As many family members as possible should participate in bringing food for the Umoja Karamu table (which is different from the table to be used during the unity ritual). Food should contain no pork, an improper food for the Umoja Karamu ceremony.

Everyone participating should be given a wooden bowl or paper plates and napkins. Earthenware cups should be used for beverages, but paper cups are acceptable.

Candlelight and incense also can be used during the ritual to establish an atmosphere of calm and reflection.

The order of your Umoja Karamu may be conducted according to the following outline:

I. Prayer
II. Libation - A liquid should be poured in honor of

ancestors who may be identified by name with each pouring.[3]

III. Reading of Narratives and Passing of Five Foods - A narrative will be read for each period. After the narrative has been read for the first period, the food representing that period will be circulated as a song from that period is presented. As the food is circulated each person will take a small portion, which will be blessed and eaten when everyone has their portion. This process will be repeated for each period.

IV. Sharing in Feast - After the Umoja Karamu table has been blessed, every one may eat from that table, while continuing in the spirit of unity and joyfulness.

Community Observance:

For observances held at churches, schools, and other community based facilities, the order of the ceremony will be the same as with the Home Observance, with three extra steps.

I. A place should be set at the Umoja Karamu table to honor the ancestors. After the ceremony is over, the food from this place setting should be placed outside to be eaten by birds and the liquid from the cup is to be poured into the earth.

II. The program should close with encouraging words of wisdom from the elders present and a benediction.

III. Food left over from the feast should be distributed to the poor or homeless.

NOTES

----

1. Dr. Ishakamusa Barashango, *Afican People and European Holidays: A Mental Genocide*, (IVth Dynasty Publishing Company, Silver Spring, Maryland, 1983) pp. 52-53

2. Ibid., pp. 53-57

3. Libation can be given at family and community functions. It should begin with a statement of respect that describes the appreciation we have for our ancestors, and the foundation that they laid for us with their lives and deaths. This would be followed by the elder leading the libation saying "for them we pour and say libation" and those attending would respond together by saying "libation." The elder will then name specific individuals that have made great contribution to the attending family, organization or African race in general. For example, the elder may say "For Steven Biko, who gave his life for the freedom struggle in Azania (South Africa) we pour and say libation" and the body would respond by again saying "libation" as the elder pours the liquid into the earth. The liquid also may be poured into a plant. The libation may end by those attending the celebration "pulling down Harambees." This is done by everyone lifting their right hand to the sky and shouting "Harambee" as they pull their hands down. This is repeated several times.

Chapter 8

Kwanzaa

(December 26 - January 1)

Kwanzaa is the most important holiday on the African American calendar. It is the most important because this observance transcends religious, ideological, regional, and class boundaries. This celebration combines elements of our African culture and African American experience to provide a framework for instilling strong values. What's more, Kwanzaa clearly represents the three dimensions important to African culture and history. The first dimension is the past, represented by the spirits of our ancestors and their collective experiences. The second dimension is the present, which is represented by our consistency in maintaining our culture and our commitment to uplift our race. The third dimension is the future represented by the children that are not yet born, the children that we hope and pray will experience real freedom in their lifetime.

Kwanzaa was founded in San Diego, CA by cultural nationalist Dr. Maulana Karenga, and was first observed in 1966. Cultural Nationalism was an important part of the 60's Black Power Movement. It was this form of nationalism that made the afro hair style, dashiki and kiswahili popular among some blacks. The word "Kwanzaa" comes from the kiswahili phrase "Matunda Ya Kwanza," which means "first fruits." Dr. Karenga added an extra "a" to "Kwanzaa" to distinguish this celebration as an African American holiday.[1] The African celebration of first fruits of the harvest is common among many African people. This African practice is done to thank the Creator for the blessing of food for the year. The Kwanzaa holiday was created by Dr. Karenga to reaffirm and restore our African heritage and culture, to introduce the Nguzo Saba, to establish a non-historic African American holiday and to serve as an annual opportunity for us to reaffirm and reinforce our bond as a people.[2]

Kwanzaa is a seven day observances from December 26th to January 1st. Throughout these seven days the Nguzo Saba, which means "the seven principles," is used to provide a value system for African Americans. The seven principles are Umoja (Unity), Kujichagulia (Self-determination), Ujima (Collective Work and Responsibility), Ujamaa (Cooperative Economics), Nia (Purpose), Kuumba (Creativity) and Imani (Faith). Each day of Kwanzaa will highlight a different principle. There are many families, schools, churches and community organizations that celebrate Kwanzaa across America. According to Cedric McClester, the author of *Kwanzaa Everything You Wanted to Know But Didn't Know Where to Ask*, there are "over 13 million Americans" that observe Kwanzaa.[3]

In many African American communities, drugs, gangs and crime have become serious problems. This has taken place largely because some youth lack proper values and principles to propel them towards righteous living. The popular observance of African American holidays will make proper values popular. It was these values that our African ancestors used to live for thousands of years in harmony with each other and the earth. These values will provide strength and courage to those that seek to change their communities.

How to Celebrate
Kwanzaa

The Kwanzaa celebration described herein was designed by Dr. Maulana Karenga, founder of Kwanzaa.

The Seven Symbols of Kwanzaa:

These symbols should be set up where Kwanzaa is to be observed before the first day of Kwanzaa. These symbols represent important values and principals in the African American culture.

1. Mkeka - A straw place mat. It symbolizes the tradition and history of the African American. All the other symbols will be placed on the Mkeka
2. Kinara - A candle holder, for the seven candles. It symbolizes the continent of Africa and our African ancestors.
3. Mazao - Fruits and vegetables. They symbolize the rewards of collective labor. Place these in a bowl on the Mkeka.
4. Muhindi - Ears of corn. They symbolize our offspring. In a home one ear of corn should be placed on the Mkeka for each child in the family.
5. Kikombe Cha Umoja - Communal unity cup. It symbolizes unity. This cup is used to make libations[4] in remembrance of our ancestors. It also may be passed around for those in attendance

to either sip from it or make a sipping gesture, to promote the spirit of oneness.

6. Zawadi - Gifts. These gifts will be shared on the seventh day of Kwanzaa (January lst). Gifts are given, usually in the immediate family, as reward for commitments that have been made and kept. In this sense, the gift serves as a reward or symbol of achievement and are not given without merit. Gift givers should avoid commercializing this aspect of Kwanzaa.

7. Mishumaa Saba - The seven candles; They symbolize the Nguzu Saba. Of the seven candles, three are green, one is black and the final three are red. Green represents hope and the Motherland, black represents our race and unity, and red represents the blood of our people. These candles are placed in the Kinara with the green on the left, black in the center and red on the right.

The Seven Days of Kwanzaa:

On each day of Kwanzaa a candle will be lit, starting with the Black (center) candle, and then from left to right on the following six days. The candle lighting should be a family or community affair and all present should participate after the meal for that day is eaten. Community forums can be held each day of Kwanzaa to highlight each principle individually. Throughout each day we extend greetings by saying "Habari gani" which means "what is the news?" The response to give when greeted with this question is the word that corresponds with that particular day. For example, if someone says "Habari gani" to you on the 3rd day, you would respond by saying "Ujima" or "Ujima, Habari gani" thereby extending the greeting to the person greeting you. Dr. Karenga defines the seven principles as follows:

1st Day - Umoja (Oo-mo-jah) - Unity, to strive for and maintain unity in the family, community, nation and race.

2nd Day - Kujichagulia (Koo-je-cha-gu-lia) - Self-determination, to define ourselves, name ourselves, create for ourselves and speak for ourselves, instead of being defined, named, created for and spoken for by others.

3rd Day Ujima (Oo-jee-mah) - Collective Work and Responsibilities, to build and maintain our community together and make our sister's and brother's problems our problems and to solve them together.

4th Day Ujamaa (Oo-ja-maa) - Cooperative Economics, to build and maintain our own stores, shops and other businesses and to profit from them together.

5th Day - Nia (Ne-ah) - Purpose, to make our collective vocation building and developing our community to restore our people to their traditional greatness.

6th Day - Kuumba (Ku-um-ba) - Creativity, to do always as much as we can, in the way we can, in order to leave our community more beautiful and beneficial than we inherited it.

7th Day - Imani (E-ma-ne) - Faith, To believe, with all our hearts, in our people, our teachers, our leaders and the righteousness and victory of our struggle.

On the evening of the 6th Day The Kwanzaa Feast of Karamu is held in the community. Those attending the feast should bring food if they are able to. This should be a time of sharing in greetings, music, reflections, public addresses, and rejoicing. At the feast libation will be made, the unity cup may be passed, the guest speaker will speak, the elders in attendance will be honored, the food will be served to all and the Mishumaa Saba will be lit. On the last day, the family should come together to share dinner. After dinner, the last candle should be lit and the family must then discuss the meaning of each of the seven principles. Lastly, the Zawadi will be given on this last day of the Kwanzaa celebration.

NOTES

----

1. Rev. Ishakamusa Barashango, *Afrikan People and European Holidays: A Mental Genocide*, Book I (IVth Dynasty Publishing Company, 1983) p. 81

2. Dr. Maulana Karenga, *The African American Holiday of Kwanzaa: A Celebration of Family, Community & Culture*, (University of Sankore Press, Los Angeles, California, 1988) p. 27

3. Cedric McClester, *Kwanzaa - Everything You Always Wanted To Know But Didn't Know Where To Ask*, (Gumbs & Thomas, New York) quote from backcover

4. For a description of libation see Chapter 7, page 69.

Appendix 1

Important Dates
in African American History

January

1st	- 1863	Emancipation Proclamation freed Blacks in rebel states
2nd	- 1831	Abolitionist paper, *The Liberator* published in Boston,
4th	- 1920	National Negro Baseball League started
	1943	William L. Dawson elected U.S. Representative, Illinois
5th	- 1943	Passing of George Washington Carver, great Scientist
6th	- 1773	Massachusetts slaves petition for freedom
8th	- 1811	Slave Revolt in New Orleans, LA
9th	- 1866	Fisk University Founded in Nashville, TN
10th	- 1864	Birth of George Washington Carver, Scientist
15th	- 1908	Alpha Kappa Alpha Sorority founded at Howard Univ.
	1929	Birth of Martin Luther King, Jr.
16th	- 1776	Enlistment of Free Blacks in the American War for Independence
18th	- 1856	Birth of Daniel Hale Williams, Surgeon and founder of Provident Hospital in Chicago, IL

1938	Cap B. Collins patented portable electric light
19th - 1775	First organized Black Baptist Church, Silver Bluff, SC.
22th - 1793	Benjamin Banneker helped plan blueprint for Washington D.C., appointed by George Washington
23rd - 1976	Passing of Paul Robeson, Actor and Activist
24th - 1885	Passing of Martin R. Delany, Doctor and Nationalist
31th - 1865	Congress passed Thirteenth Amendment abolishing slavery

February
(Black History Month, began as Negro History Week by Carter G. Woodson in 1926)

1st - 1865	John S. Rock was first Black to practice before the U.S. Supreme Court
4th - 1822	Freed Blacks from U.S. settled in Liberia
5th - 1934	Birth of Hank Aaron, Baseball Legend
10th - 1780	Seven blacks challenge taxation without representation
12th - 1909	NAACP Founded in responds to 1908 Springfield, IL riot
13th - 1746	Birth of Absalom Jones, first Black Protestant Minister
1923	*The Renaissance*, first Black professional basketball team organized

14th - 1817   Birth of Frederick Douglass, Abolitionist and Orator

      1867   Augusta Institute, now Morehouse College, opened in Atlanta, GA.

15th - 1957   Southern Christian Leadership Conference organized

16th - 1874   Frederick Douglass elected President of Freedmen's Bank & Trust Co.

20th - 1895   Passing of Frederick Douglass

21st - 1936   Birth of Barbara Jordan, Lawyer and Congresswoman

      1965   Passing of Malcolm X (El Hajj Malik El Shabazz) by assassination

22nd - 1911   Passing of Frances Ellen Watkins Harper, Poet and first Black woman to have full length novel published

23rd - 1868   Birth of W.E.B. DuBois

25th - 1870   Hiram Revels elected first Black to U.S. Senate

      1964   Cassius Clay (Muhammad Ali) beat Sonny Liston winning the Heavyweight title

27th - 1988   Debi Thomas won medal at Winter Olympics

28th - 1784   Passing of Phyllis Wheatley, Poet and Freedom Fighter

March

1st   - 1875   President Grant signed a Civil Rights Law prohibiting racial discrimination in public accommodations

2nd - 1867 Howard University was chartered
3rd - 1865 The Freedman's Bureau was established
4th - 1875 Blanch Bruce elected U.S. Senator, Mississippi, also, Birth of Garrett A. Morgan, Inventor of the traffic signal and gas mask
5th - 1770 Passing of Crispus Attucks, first to die for American independence from British
6th - 1857 Dred Scott decision states that American Blacks have no rights that whites are required to respect
7th - 1539 Estevanica (Esteban) explored southwestern part of U.S. and became first non-Native American to enter New Mexico
8th - 1876 Senate refused to seat P.B.S. Pinchback
10th - 1910 Robert L. Vann founded *The Pittsburgh Courier*
         1913 Passing of Harriet Tubman, great Leader
12th - 1955 Passing of Charlie "Bird" Parker, Jazz Legend
13th - 1865 Bill allowing slaves to serve in Confederate Army
14th - 1977 Passing of Fannie Lou Hamer, Voting Rights Heroine
16th - 1827 *Freedom's Journal*, first Black paper founded
17th - 1896 C.B. Scott patented the street sweeper
20th - 1883 Jan Matzeliger patented shoe lasting machine
22nd - 1965 Selma to Mongomery March Began

26th - 1872   Thomas J. Martin patented the fire
             extinguisher
     1911   William H. Lewis became U.S. Assistant
             Attorney General
28th - 1914   Sol Butler set track record
30th - 1870   Fifteenth Amendment ratified giving
             blacks voting rights

April

1st - 1950   Passing of Dr. Charles Drew, Inventor of
             blood plasma
3rd - 1950   Passing of Carter G. Woodson, great
             Historian
4th - 1928   Birth of Maya Angelou, author, Poet and
             Playwright
     1968   Passing of Martin Luther King, Jr. by
             assassination
5th - 1856   Birth of Booker T. Washington, Educator
6th - 1909   Matthew Henson, first man to reach the
             North Pole
7th - 1915   Birth of Billie Holiday, great Blues Singer
8th - 1974   Hank Aaron set new home run record,
             after receiving more than 500 letters
             threatening his life and family for
             seeking to break Babe Ruths home run
             record
9th - 1866   Civil Rights Bill passed to protect freed
             Blacks from The Black Codes and
             other oppressive laws
     1898   Birth of Paul Robeson, Actor and Activist

12th - 1983   Harold Washington Elected Mayor of Chicago, IL

15th - 1960   Student Nonviolent Coordinating Committee formed at Shaw University

19th - 1775   Black minutemen fight at Lexington & Concord in the War for Independence

20th - 1866   Fisk University opened in Nashville, TN

23rd - 1856   Birth of Granville T. Woods, great Inventor

29th - 1899   Birth of Edward Kennedy "Duke" Ellington, Big Band Legend

May

1st - 1867   Howard University chartered by Congress

4th - 1897   J. H. Smith patents lawn sprinkler

6th - 1812   Birth of Martin R. Delany, Doctor and Nationalist

1960   Civil Rights Act protecting the rights of citizens

1988   Eugene A. Marino became America's first Black Roman Catholic Archbishop

7th - 1878   J.R. Winter, patented the first fire escape ladder

8th - 1925   Brotherhood of Sleeping Car Porters founded by Asa Phillip Randolph

12th - 1871   "Sit In" protest staged in Louisville, KY.

17th - 1954   Supreme Court school segregation decision

18th - 1896 Plessy vs. Ferguson decision establishing "separate but equal" public accommodations

1955 Passing of Mary McLeod Bethune

19th - 1925 Birth of Malcolm X (El Hajj Malik El Shabazz)

20th - 1958 Robert N.C. Nix elected to Congress, PA

24th - 1974 Passing of Edward Kennedy "Duke" Ellington

26th - 1965 Voting Rights Bill passed outlawing grandfather clauses, literacy test and other repressive laws

June

3rd - 1884 Granville T. Woods patents steam boiler furnace

1904 Birth of Dr. Charles Drew, Doctor invented blood plasma

6th - 1790 Jean Baptiste Pointe Dusable became first to settle where Chicago now stands

1930 Dillard University founded in New Orleans, LA

7th - 1892 G.T. Sampson patents clothe dryer

1917 Birth of Gwendolyn Brooks, Pulitzer Prize winner for poetry and Illinois Poet Laureate

1943 Birth of Nikki Giovanni, great Poet

9th - 1904 James C. Napier founded the first Black owned bank

10th - 1794   Richard Allen started the Independent
              Methodist Movement
      1940   Passing of Marcus Mosiah Garvey,
              Nationalist and Great Leader
llth - 1911 Marcus Garvey founded the Universal
              Negro Improvement Association
12th - 1963 Passing of Medgar Evers by assassination
              in Mississippi
14th - 1970 Chris Dickerson wins "Mr. America"
21st - 1821 African Methodist Epistcopal Zion
              Church held its first yearly conference
              in New York City
22th - 1938 Joe Louis defeated Max Schmeling For
              Heavyweight title
27th - 1919 Marcus Garyey's Universal Negro
              Improvement Association incorporated
              the Black Star Line (ships) of Deleware
30th - 1917 Birth of Lena Horne, great Entertainer

July

2nd   - 1872 Elijah J. McCoy patented the "real
              McCoy" lubricator cup
9th   - 1966 NAACP dissociates from "Black Power"
              doctrine
10th - 1875 Birth of Mary McLeod Bethune, founder
              of the Daytona School For Girls which
              merged with Cookman Institute to
              form Bethune-Cookman College

1893   Daniel Hale Williams performed first modern day open heart surgery at Provident Hospital in Chicago, IL

11th - 1905   Niagara Movement was organized by W.E.B. DuBois and dissolved in 1907 due to internal conflicts

13th - 1787   Slavery banned in Northwest Territory

14th - 1834   Henry Blair patented the corn harvester

16th - 1862   Birth of Ida B. Wells, led anti-lynching law fight

17th - 1862   Congress passed the Militia Act allowing Blacks to fight in the Union Army

18th - 1905   Granville T. Woods patented the railway brake

19th - 1919   Race riots in Washington, D.C. began when mobs of whites killed blacks for alleged attacks on white women

20th - 1957   Althea Gibson won Women's Single Championship at Wimbledon

21st - 1896   National Association of Colored Women organized

23rd - 1891   Birth of Louis T. Wrights pioneer in antibiotic research

27th - 1919   Race riots kill hundreds in Chicago, IL after whites murder a Black man for swimming across an imaginary color line at a public beach

28th - 1868   Fourteenth Amendment ratified giving blacks citizenship

30th - 1945   Adam Clayton Powell, elected to Congress

August

1st	- 1920	25,000 people attend the first International Convention of Negroes, held by the Universal Negro Improvement Association at Madison Square Garden New York City
2nd	- 1850	William Still started Underground Railroad
4th	- 1896	W.S. Grant patented curtain rod
10th	- 1989	General Colin Powell nominated Chairman of the Joint Chiefs of Staff
14th	- 1883	Birth of Ernest E. Just, leading Biological Scientist
17th	- 1887	Birth of Marcus Mosiah Garvey, great Nationalist Leader
19th	- 1884	M.C. Harvey patented lantern
20th	- 1619	20 Africans were brought to Jamestown
21st	- 1831	Nat Turner led slave revolt killing 55 whites in Southampton, Virginia
	1904	Birth of William "Count" Basie, Jazz Legend
23rd	- 1892	O.E. Brown patented horseshoe
26th	- 1920	Birth of Charlie "Bird" Parker, Jazz Legend
27th	- 1963	Passing of W.E.B. DuBois, Author and Educator
28th	- 1963	March On Washington
31st	- 1836	Henry Blair patented the cotton planting machine

September

5th	- 1877	"Pap" Singleton founded "Singleton's Colony, Kansas" as a Black settlement
6th	- 1800	James Durham was first Black recognized doctor
8th	- 1981	Passing of Roy Wilkins, Civil Rights Activist
9th	- 1915	Association for the Study of Negro Life & History was organized by Carter G. Woodson
12th	- 1787	First African American Masonic Lodge organized
15th	- 1963	Four girls killed in bombing of church, Birmingham, AL.
17th	- 1983	Venessa Williams wins "Miss America"
19th	- 1881	Tuskegee Institute opened by Booker T. Washington
20th	- 1830	First Negro National Convention
22th	- 1950	Ralphe J. Bunche awarded Nobel Peace Prize
23rd	- 1926	Birth of John Coltrane, Jazz Legend
28th	- 1895	National Baptist Convention organized

October

2nd	- 1800	Birth of Nat Turner, Visionary and Revolutionist
4th	- 1864	New Orleans Tribune, a Black daily, began publication

7th - 1800 Passing of Gabriel Prosser by execution
             for leading a slave revolt
      1897   Birth of the Honorable Elijah
             Muhammad, Muslim Leader
8th - 1941 Birth of Jesse L. Jackson, Sr., Civil Rights
             Leader
9th - 1869 Morgan State College opened
10th - 1974 Violence erupts in Boston over busing
             issue
11th - 1964 Martin Luther Kings Jr. was given the
             Nobel Peace Prize
12th - 1925 Xavier University Founded in New
             Orleans, LA
16th - 1859 John Brown attack on Harper Ferry
21st - 1850 Chicago refused to enforce Fugitive Slave
             Law
23rd - 1947 NAACP petitioned U.N. on racial
             injustices
24th - 1972 Passing of Jackie Robinson, Baseball
             Legend
26th - 1911 Birth of Mahalia Jackson, great Singer
30th - 1954 Black units abolished in armed forces
      1966   Black Panther Party formed in
             Oakland, CA.

November

7th - 1989 Douglas Wilder elected Governor of
             Virginia
8th - 1966 Edward W. Brook elected to U.S. Senate
             from Mass.

9th - 1731 Birth of Benjamin Banneker, made first
American made clock

      1868 Howard University Medical School
opened

10th - 1891 Granville T. Woods patented electric
railway

11th - 1831 Passing of Nat Turner by hanging for
leading slave revolt killing slave owners
and their families

12th - 1977 Ernest N. "Dutch" Morial elected Mayor
of New Orleans

13th - 1839 First anti-slavery political party, the
Liberty Party, was organized

14th - 1977 Trial began for 1963 Birmingham church
bombing which killed four girls and
spark rioting

18th - 1787 Birth of Sojourner Truth, Orator for
freedom

20th - 1923 Garrett A. Morgan patented traffic light

21st - 1865 Shaw University Founded

22nd - 1930 Lost Found Nation of Islam in the
Wilderness of North America was
founded in Detroit, MI

23rd - 1897 J.L. Love patented pencil sharpener and
Andrew Jackson Beard patented the
Automatic Railroad Car Coupler,
commonly called the "Jenny" Coupler

26th - 1883 Passing of Sojourner Truth, Orator for
freedom

      1911 Birth of Mahalia Jackson, Gospel Music
Legend

29th - 1905 *Chicago Defender* newspaper started

December

1st	- 1955	Rosa Parks sparked Montgomery bus boycott by refusing to give her seat to a white man
2nd	- 1859	Passing of John Brown by execution for insurrection
3rd	- 1847	Frederick Douglass published first "*North Star*"
8th	- 1925	Birth of Sammy Davis, Jr.
10th	- 1846	Norbert Rillieux patented sugar making equipment
11th	- 1872	P.B.S. Pinchback bacame Acting Governor of Louisiana
16th	- 1976	Andrew Young appointed Ambassador to the U.N.
19th	- 1875	Birth of Carter G. Woodson, great Historian
21st	- 1920	W.H. Sammons patented the hair straightening comb
23rd	- 1867	Birth of Madam C.J. Walker, first Millionaire Business-women in America
26th	- 1908	Jack Johnson became first Black Heavyweight Champion
	1966	First observance of Kwanzaa (first fruits), created by Maulana Karenga

Appendix 2

Historic Origin of Popular American Holidays

New Year's Day

Observed January 1st; The beginning of the new year has changed from time to time but throughout the world celebration of the new year has been observed since the beginning of recorded history.

Valentine's Day

St. Valentine was either a Christian priest or bishop in Rome about A.D. 270. He was ordered to be executed by the Emperor Claudius II for conducting illegal marriage ceremonies. He is said to have become close friends with the jailor's daughter and left a note for her on the day of his execution signed "Your Valentine."

St. Patrick's Day

Began in celebration of Patrick, who was taken into Ireland as a slave about A.D. 405 and later escaped. After receiving religious training in monasteries he returned to Ireland in A.D. 432 as a Christian missionary and is credited with bringing Christianity to Ireland.

Easter

Though it is observed as the celebration of the crucifixion and resurrection of Jesus Christ, it originally began as a day traditionally set aside as a pagan observance of the Earth's awakening or spring. Also as a celebration of the God of Spring Adonis who is said to have died and risen from the dead. The word Easter is derived from the name of the Goddess of Spring Eostre. It is from this tradition that we get the Easter egg symbolizing new life and the hare (Easter bunny) which was sacred to Eostre. About the third century the Christian Church added it's symbolism to this observance.

Fourth of July

Observed as the birthday of America and the remembrance of America gaining independence from Britain.

Halloween

Originally called All Hallow's Eve, the night before All Saint's Day. October 31st was observed as the eve of the Celtic New Year. At this time a festival was held celebrating Samhain, Lord of Death, who would call together the souls of the wicked that were condemned to inherit the bodies of animals, especially cats. The custom of wearing disguises is done to imitate the walking dead, witches, and possessed animals that would roam the earth. Halloween is still the most sacred day among witches, despite the religious flavor given to it by Pope Gregory in the eigth century in honor of Catholic saints.

Thanksgiving

Generally celebrated as a time of giving thanks to God for blessings and for protecting the Pilgrims through their first winter. Of the 102 original Pilgrims, forty-four died and most of those that remained were either sick or mentally ill. Some of them resorted to cannibalism to survive. Having survived winter, famine, sickness and death, it was the help of one Patuxet, named Squanto that kept them all from dying. Though the Pilgrims and indigenous people shared in a feast in 1622 to celebrate their first harvest, we must note that the very first official Thanksgiving Day was proclaimed by the Governor of Massachusetts Bay Colony in 1637 to celebrate the massacre of 700 indigenous (called "Indian") men, women and children in a violent attack on their tribe.

Christmas

Generally Celebrated as the Birth of Jesus Christ. At least 2000 years before Christ the ancient Kemites (or Egyptians) began to celebrate December 25th as the birth of the sun god Horus, son of Isis and Osiris. The Persian version of Horus was called Mithra, also a halo wearing sun god. During the third century A.D., many citizens of the Roman Empire conducted the Feast of Saturnalia, which honored Mithra on December 25th. The Christian Church considered observance of the festival so popular that they could not outlaw it and decided to transform the festival and its rituals by adding Christian symbolism. Despite Christian influence, pagan symbols remain popular during Christmas, such as the Christmas tree, mistletoe, yule log, Christmas lights, chimney, and even Santa.

BIBLIOGRAPHY AND ORGANIZATION LISTING

Books:

Barashango, Dr. Ishakamusa. *African People and European Holiday: A Mental Genocide*, (IVth Dynasty Publishing Company, Silver Spring, - Maryland, 1983)

Bennett, Lerone Jr. *Before the Mayflower: A History of the Negro in America 1619-1964*, (Penguin Books Ltd, New York, New York, 1976)

Blassingame, John W. *The Slave Community*, (Oxford University Press, New York, 1975)

Davidson, Basil, *The African Slave Trade*, (Atlantic-Little, Brown and Company, Boston/ Toronto, 1980)

Genovese, Eugene D. *Roll, Jordan, Roll*, (Random House, Inc., New York, 1976)

Green, Victor. *Festival and Saints Days*, (Blandford Press Ltd., Poole Dorset, Britain, 1978)

Haley, Alex and Malcolm X. *Autobiography of Malcolm X*, (Grove-Press, New York, 1964)

Jackson, Jesse L.., Sr. *Straight From The Heart*, (Fortress Press, Philidelphia, 1987)

Karenga, Dr. Maulana. *The African American Holiday of Kwanzaa: A Celebration of Family, Community & Culture*, (University of Sankore Press, Los Angeles, California, 1988)

Mazrui, Ali A. *The Africans*, (Little, Brown and Company, Boston and Toronto, 1986)

McClester, Cedric. *Kwanzaa - Everything You Always Wanted To Know But Didn't Know Where To Ask*, (Gumbs and Thomas, New York, 1990)

McFarland, Daniel Miles. *Historical Dictionary of Ghana*, (The Scarecrow Press, Inc. Metuchen, N.J., and London, 1985)

Nkrumah, Kwame. *Africa Must Unite*, (International Publishers, New York, 1970)

Shannon-Thornberry, Milo. *The Alternate Celebrations Catalogue*, (The Pilgrim Press, New York, 1982)

Stuckey, Sterling. *Slave Culture*, (Oxford University Press, New York, 1987)

Van Sertima, Ivan and Clifton E. Marsh. *Great Black Leaders: Ancient and Modern*, (Journal of African Civilization Ltd., Inc., 1988)

Washington, Booker T. *Up From Slavery*, (A Bantom Book/Published by arrangement with Doubleday and Company, Inc., 1977)

Wiggins, William H., Jr. *O Freedom! Afro-American Emancipation Celebrations*, (University of Tennessee Press)

Williams, Eric. *Capitalism and Slavery*, (University of North Carolina Press, 1944)

Periodicals:

Journal of Negro History, "Annual Report of The Director" by Carter G. Woodson, October 1927

Negro Digest, "Historic Afro-American Holidays" by Benjamin Quarles, February 1967

New Republic, "Uneasy Holiday" by Taylor Branch, February 3, 1986

Newsweek, "Behind The King Debate" by David M. Alpern with Gloria Borger, October 31, 1983

Phylon, "The John Canoe Festival" by Ira De A. Reid, Fourth Quarter 1942

Organization Listing:

All-African People Revolutionary Party
P.O. Box 43624
Washington, D.C. 20010

Association for the Study of
  Afro-American Life and History
1407 14th Street, N.W.
Washington, D.C. 20005-3704
(202) 667-2822

Martin Luther King, Jr. Federal Holiday Commission
449 Auburn Avenue N.E.
Atlanta, Georgia 30312
(404) 730-3155

  (Washington, D.C. address)
  451 7th Street, S.W.
  Washington, D.C. 20410
  (202) 708-1005

National Black United Front
700 East Oakwood Blvd
Chicago, IL 60653 (312) 268-7500 Ext. 144

National Malcolm X Commemoration Commission
c/o Ron Daniels
P.O. Box 5641
Youngstown, Oh 44504
(216) 746-5747

AFRICAN AMERICAN HOLIDAYS
CELEBRATION KITS

Order form

The items listed below should be used according to the instructions provided for celebrating African American Holidays. Identify the items you want by circling it's item-number on the order form.

Item #

#1	Happy Birthday Martin Luther King Jr. Poster	$7.00
#2	Rites of Passage Guidelines	$1.00
#3	Malcolm X Commemoration Poster	$7.00
#4	Free South Africa Poster	$7.00
#5	Red, Black & Green Flag	$25.00
#6	Copy of the Emanicipation Proclamation	$1.00
#7	Umoja Karamu Five Narratives	$3.00
#8	Mkeka (Straw Mat)	$8.00
#9	Kinara (Candle Holder)	$20.00
#10	Mishumaa Saba (Set of Seven Candles)	$7.00
#11	Nguzu Saba Poster	$7.00
#12	African American Holidays Yearly Calender	$4.00
#13	Kente Cloth	$30.00
#14	Special Celebration Kit (All Items Listed Above)	$100.00

Indicate how many items ordered in the space beside each item-number.

Item #:

1_____   2_____   3_____   4_____   5_____   6_____   7_____

8_____   9_____   10_____   11_____   12_____   13_____   14_____

NAME _____

CH./ORG./BUS./SCH. _____

ADDRESS _____

CITY/ST/ZIP _____

PHONES (D)(   )_____ (E)(   )_____

Please send _____ copies of
AFRICAN AMERICAN HOLIDAYS ($7.95/each)

Total Ordered $_____
(Including copies
  of **African American Holidays**)

Shipping and Handling $_____
  (6% of each order)

TOTAL ENCLOSED $_____
(Check or Money Order)   _____

(Orders are shipped UPS. All prices are subject to change without notice. Allow 2-4 weeks for delivery. Rush orders are extra. For more information (312) 548-6000.)

Mail To:

Popular Truth, Inc.
334 East 37th Street
Chicago, IL 60653-1346

(312) 548-6000